THE BOOMER'S GUIDE TO RECOVERING YOUR LOST RETIREMENT:

The Bill Fisher Story

By

MICHAEL R. BURNS

Acknowledgements

I would like to acknowledge several people who assisted me with the content, editing, and production that made this book possible.

First and foremost, I would like to posthumously thank Bill Fisher for his knowledge and inspiration that motivated me to tell his story and investment philosophy.

I would also like to thank my wife, Robin, who contributed to the content immeasurably and encouraged me to continue writing, even though there were times when I wanted to give up. She was a true inspiration and motivated me to complete the project.

Next, I would like to thank Lisa Fisher, my sister-in-law, and Staci Burns, my daughter, who helped by contributing ideas and editing the manuscript extensively. Also on the list are other Fisher family members, including Bill Fisher, Lisa Fisher, John Fisher, Sally Fisher, Katie Grabill, and David Fischer. The entire Fisher family helped by contributing content to the Zany Bill Fisherisms, (Resource Center, Item Q), which are quotes that we all heard and laughed about for many years. Bill Fisher was a very bright man and said many unusual things that were not only funny but that usually had great meaning and taught a lesson as well.

Finally, I would like to give credit to Tiffany Dean of Smith & Dean, Inc. and Steve Lillo of PlanetLink, for their creative contributions to the graphics and the website design. Both parties were a pleasure to work with and very professional and diligent in their approach to the project.

Table of Contents

Disclaimer

The Bill Fisher Story was written by me, Mike Burns, an average working-class son-in-law who had the privilege of knowing and observing Bill Fisher for twenty-seven years. I have no formal training in investment strategy or financial planning, nor do I have any financial or broker licenses of any kind.

What I do have is twenty-seven years of learning from Bill Fisher, who also had no training in investment strategy or financial planning, except for an old insurance license from the State of Kansas.

Bill Fisher was a very intelligent man. He was well-read and possessed a tremendous memory. He had a keen wit and loved to tell us stories, relate funny jokes, and give us serious advice. His practical knowledge was there for the taking, and my wife and I soaked it up.

Each family member realized we had to work hard to succeed in this world. We knew that no one would part the clouds and hand us a pot of money. Bill Fisher taught us that becoming successful was a daily grind, much like Major League Baseball, where the players have one hundred and fifty-five games each season. You have to show up every day and give it your best, no matter how bad you are feeling. "Life — and becoming successful — is a marathon, not a sprint," Bill used to say.

Bill taught us about setting goals, conservative investing, entrepreneurship, and the thrills and setbacks of running your own business. He was an inspiration to the whole family, and I felt that he might inspire you, too. So, here is *The Bill Fisher Story*. Bill always said, "It is never too late to start over!"

THE BILL FISHER STORY

The Boomer's Guide to Recovering Your Lost Retirement

BILL'S STORY

The great recession of 2008–2010 practically wiped out half of Baby Boomers' retirement money—money they had saved over a lifetime. This is a sobering fact, and many Boomers were dismayed and angry at the series of economic disasters that pummeled their nest eggs and hammered their net worth. Now that we have survived the worst of the downturn and are still standing, what should the Boomers do to reverse this downward trend and start to build back their retirement money?

Before we get into the specific recommendations and how tos, I would like to relate the story of my father-in-law,

Bill Fisher, and how he, at age seventy-two, started saving and investing from scratch and ended up with a net worth of $1 million.

Bill Fisher was born in Denver, on October 28, 1916. He had curly blond hair, and although his given name was James Richard Fisher, his maid nicknamed him Billy, and the name stuck. Soon after Bill was born, his family moved to Kansas City, Kansas.

His upper-middle-class family provided an excellent upbringing, until his father died, when Bill was only ten. Bill's life changed. The family no longer had someone to rely upon for financial support. Everyone in the family had to go to work just to make ends meet. The family eventually survived and Bill took on his father's responsibilities and became the head of the household.

The family muddled along for several years and, during World War II, Bill graduated from high school, and eventually enlisted in the US Air Force. Bill served his country in England, and when the war was over, he came home to Kansas City.

In 1951, Bill met and fell in love with Catherine Larraine Knaub of Chicago. They soon married and settled in Kansas City. They had four children, two sons and two daughters — one of whom I married in 1984.

In the early years of Bill's family life, he started an appliance store, Reliance Appliance, and became fairly successful selling Kitchen-Aid products, washers and dryers, and other accessories for the local community. His business thrived, and he was able to provide for his family in a generous way.

Everything came up roses for Bill and his family for ten years, but then a terrible catastrophe occurred. Bill's appliance store burned down. To make matters worse, he discovered that his insurance policy had not been renewed, and he was left with nothing.

Bill was devastated. He had been pouring all his money into the business and his family. He didn't have a savings plan, pension, or income to support his family. Consequently, Bill became depressed and stayed at home for several years. He eventually obtained an insurance license, but he never fully recovered from the loss of both the business and his self-esteem.

The family muddled through these years. The kids had to attend a public school, and Bill's wife had to go back to work as a secretary for a company in downtown Kansas City. Finally, it hit Bill that he had to go back to work somewhere just to start bringing in a consistent income for the household. The kids were now in college, and the family's expenses had grown considerably.

At fifty-nine, Bill took a job as an entry-level customer service representative for a telecommunications company. The family now had two incomes, so they could pay their expenses, and Bill had something to do every day.

Bill continued to work at the company until 1986, when he turned seventy. At that time, federal law dictated that seventy was the mandatory retirement age. Consequently, Bill was "fired" or mandatorily retired from the communications company. Bill did not want to retire. He liked his job, his income and the companionship of his peers at work.

About this time, President Reagan had been elected, and he passed a law that made it illegal to discriminate against anyone because of age. Therefore, Bill hired an attorney and filed a lawsuit against his former company because of age discrimination. Bill won.

Now, at seventy, Bill was reinstated to his position with his company, and he resumed working. Bill now had eleven years of service with the company, and he had become eligible for a company pension.

Bill's wife, Catherine, or "Larrie" as friends and family called her, suffered from heart disease and diabetes, and in 1988, she passed away from a sudden heart attack.

Although heartbroken, Bill continued to work and relied upon his family, friends, and coworkers for support. It was at this point in Bill's life, at age seventy-two, that he started investing his extra money. He received $50,000 from Larrie's life insurance policy, so this made a nice beginning for his investments. *It should be noted that if you ever receive an inheritance or some sort of financial payout, you should invest that money!* Most people spend the majority of this newly acquired money, and before they know it, there is nothing left to invest. It is all gone.

At this time, Bill was making around $50,000 per year at his job. He was also getting $3,300 per month in Social Security payments. Bill had waited until age seventy to file for his Social Security and therefore received the maximum benefit. If he had filed for Social Security at sixty-two, his benefits would only have been $1,200 per month. Bill was also receiving around $700 from his company pension, having now worked for his company for thirteen years. So at age seventy-two, Bill was bringing in a gross income of $8,166 per month. After taxes, this mounted to about $5,389 per month.

With the kids grown, self-sufficient, and out of the house; with his thirty-year mortgage now paid; and with very little expense for himself, Bill suddenly found himself with a lot of extra cash on hand. This point in Bill's life was the beginning of his financial renaissance.

Initially, Bill started buying his company's stock. It paid a good dividend, and he would buy shares from his friends at work without having to pay a broker's commission. Over the next several years, Bill accumulated about $30,000 in his company's stock, which paid him around $1,400 in dividends each year.

Over the next twelve years, Bill continued to work at his company, until he was eighty-four, when he finally retired. Bill passed away at ninety-three, having lived a long and fruitful life and raising four great children, all of whom became successful and productive members of society.

Between the ages of seventy-two and ninety-two, Bill invested in stocks, municipal bonds, Dividend Reinvestment Programs (DRIPs), and residential rental property until he had amassed a net worth of $1 million. It is true that a portion of his stock did get whacked in the 2008 recession, but it was rebounding nicely at the time of his death.

As I reviewed Bill Fisher's life, it suddenly became apparent to me that he was a great poster boy for someone who started from scratch at a later age in life and built a net worth of $1 million with very little difficulty and while still enjoying life to the fullest. Bill spent his later years traveling overseas to several countries and living the country club life.

I had always been a great admirer of Bill Fisher and his wisdom in the twenty-seven years that I knew him. I knew he could be a good role model for my family and me, and for other Baby Boomers who are wondering what to do in this time of economic upheaval and uncertainty. Therefore, I have analyzed his investment philosophy and divided it into a three-pronged strategy that anyone can easily follow.

It should be noted that anyone of any age can start this retirement investment strategy. Actually, the younger you are, the more years you have to accumulate wealth. So, if you are just starting out in your twenties, you should be able to build a net worth of a few million dollars. However, I especially want to emphasize the point that it is never too late to start investing, and *The Bill Fisher Story* illustrates this point dramatically.

GETTING STARTED

When you evaluate your current circumstances, it is important that you have enough income each month to pay for your living expenses. If you cannot cover your expenses each month, then you have to increase your income and reduce your expenses. You cannot save or invest any money each month until you have a surplus of money available to invest. You may have to make some hard choices, like taking on a second job or cutting back on your expenses, like club fees, expensive restaurants, and new cars. You and I are not the federal government. We cannot go into debt every month and expect to continue our current spending without paying any consequences. Eventually, the people we owe money to will foreclose on our assets or push us into bankruptcy. This is not a very pretty picture.

If you need help getting your spending and budget under control, I recommend that you read Dave Ramsey's books, listen to his radio show each day, and/or take one of his financial courses. He has a wonderful plan on how to cut your expenses and get your credit card debt under control.

Suze Orman is another budget master who gives excellent advice on how to manage and control your budget. She has a TV show on CNBC, and she has written several books. (See "Resource Center, Item C" for Dave's information and "Item P" for Suze's information.)

Another point is that if you are already retired or out of work, now is the time to dust off the resume, start interviewing, and get a job! At first, any job will do; just get something to start bringing in more money so that you can start building your net worth again. You can always trade up and get a better job or one that you actually like and that, I hope, pays more money.

This point is important for a number of reasons. Of course, the new job will start bringing revenue into your life, but it is very important to note that the job can also be very good for your mental health. It is productive, it can give you improved self-esteem, and it gives you stimulation from your peers. In other words, it will be good for you emotionally and socially. You also may receive insurance benefits, which will cut down on your health care costs, plus provide you better coverage.

I hear about people who have given up in today's world. They no longer look for work, and they sit on the couch and read the paper or watch television. They say they will just get by on Social Security and live a simple life. This doesn't work! These people have sentenced themselves to avoiding success. Just get started! Get a job as a retail store greeter or a customer service representative. Look online and use social media, such as Craigslist, LinkedIn, or Facebook. Don't be afraid to ask people for a job. The main thing is to become active again.

Another option for bringing in more money is to become an agent for a company, selling their products or services over the phone from your home or apartment. This way, you can become your own boss and work the hours that you want to work. Some of the industries that utilize agents are telecommunications, utilities, Internet, insurance, and real estate. The latter two industries require licenses, but you can make significant sums of money in these industries if you dedicate yourself to them full time.

If you choose the agent option, you can form a company and write off the expenses of your business from your home. Of course, you have to make some money from your business or the Internal Revenue Service might deem your business a hobby and deny your expense deductions.

As an agent who sells a company's products/services, you can learn the art of selling through telephone calls (telemarketing), Internet marketing (websites), and e-mail marketing. You can also use LinkedIn to join specific groups and establish relationships that can result in sales. In addition, you can recruit subagents who sell for you (you and your subagent share in the commissions). Check "Resource Section, Item A" in the back of the book for a list of companies that offer an agent program. You can also check in "Resource Section, Item M" for a sample agent agreement in the conference calling industry. "Resource Section, Item N" also has materials, including a script and rebuttals, that will help you succeed at selling conference calling over the phone.

Another good option for those of you who want to work out of your home is writing content for the Internet. You can write books, like this one, and publish them on www. amazon.com. If you price them under $9.99, you can receive 70 percent of all the sales generated from the Amazon website. You can also write blogs and articles for the Internet on different topics that you like and understand. You can then publish them on websites, either your own website or other publishing sites, that will allow you to generate an audience (list), and then you can market related products/services to that audience for a new source of revenue.

When you have enough money coming in each month to cover your expenses plus some money left over for investments, one of the main rules to remember is this: *Never lend money to family and friends for investment opportunities!* I know this is a hard rule to follow, especially if you have an immediate family member with this great idea for a new company or get-rich-quick scheme. I promise you that if you give someone your hard-earned money, you will never see it again. You can kiss it goodbye.

I have learned this lesson the hard way myself. I am embarrassed to tell you how much money I have frittered away on promising "sound-good" investments that never saw the light of day and that lost all of everyone's money. About fifteen years ago, I realized that my wife was my best partner, and we promised ourselves that we should invest in each other. We count on ourselves to become successful. We don't blindly throw money at someone else's idea and allow that person to drive the project into the ditch. When you give your money away to others, you lose the control of the outcome.

After you have your budget under control, another important point is to build yourself an emergency fund, which should be composed of around one year's salary. This emergency fund should be liquid so that you can use it if you truly have an emergency. This fund is your safety net, and it is as important as any other investment.

SOCIAL SECURITY

In order to receive Social Security payments each month when you retire, you must have worked for forty quarters or ten years during which you and your employer contributed to the Social Security fund. The government takes out 6.2 percent of your wages each check for Social Security. Your company also contributes another 6.2 percent to the Social Security fund on your behalf.

If you have met the above requirements, then you can file for Social Security benefits anytime after you turn sixty-two. If you file at this age, then you will receive the lowest amount of money payable from the Social Security fund, or about $1,200 per month. If you wait until you are seventy to file, you will receive the maximum amount of Social Security each month, or around $3,300 per month. If you file somewhere in between your sixty-second and seventieth birthdays, you will receive a proportionate amount of money between these two monthly amounts. Check "Resource Section, Item O" in the back of this book for the Social Security Administration website link. *The important point to* *note is that if you are healthy and working from ages sixty-two through seventy, you should wait to file for Social Security benefits until after your seventieth birthday, which will allow you to earn the maximum of $3,300 per month in Social Security benefits.* This benefit will be paid to you monthly for the rest of your life. You will have taxes taken out, but as long as you are working or making enough money to cover your expenses, the net sum will be available for investing in your nest egg! Remember the Bill Fisher story.

INDIVIDUAL RETIREMENT ACCOUNTS (IRAS)

The federal government established IRAs as a way for individuals to put aside money for their retirement each year, with the benefit of not having the money taxed until they take it out of the account. According to tax laws at the time of this writing, if you are under fifty, as an individual you may put up to $5,000 annually into an IRA. This money is invested through your bank or brokerage, and it can be put into Certificates of Deposit (CDs), stocks, bonds, mutual funds, or an assortment of different investments. This $5,000 is tax deductible in the year you place it into your IRA. *I recommend placing this retirement money into safe mutual funds!*

If you are over fifty, the maximum IRA contribution jumps to $6,000. Therefore, you can write off the $6,000 for each year that you make this IRA contribution.

Everyone should contribute to an IRA each year to the maximum limit! You should follow this rule for two main reasons: First, your contribution each year is tax deductible; second, all of the interest, dividends, and growth that appreciate in your IRA are tax deferred. You do not have to pay taxes on any of the money while you are in the IRA. You have to pay taxes only when you pull money out of your IRA. The government has a formula that requires you to take out so much money from your IRA each year when you reach seventy. Check "Resource Section, Item F" in the back of the book for the government website link.

401(K) ACCOUNTS

A 401(k) is a retirement account that you can establish through the company you work for or, if you are self-employed, on your own. If you work for a company that offers a 401(k) plan, become familiar with it and how you can participate in it. The plan typically allows you to contribute monthly sums of money out of your check to this retirement account. The plan will usually have several options on how the plan will invest your money, such as mutual funds, bonds, and other investment options. *I recommend placing this retirement money into safe mutual funds!*

Sometimes, your company will match a portion of your contributions, giving you an even greater retirement account. The good feature of the 401(k) retirement account is that all of your earnings in this account are tax-free until you start taking them out. *Remember that if you have the chance, always participate in a 401(k) because you can build wealth without having the burden of paying taxes while you are in the plan!*

HIGH-DIVIDEND STOCKS

Once you have covered your living expenses with income from your job(s), you now have the freedom to start investing the remainder of your income into investments. You should first invest any excess income each month in your IRA and your 401(k) retirement funds. After those funds are maxed out, you can move on to the other options for building back your retirement money.

To have a balanced and diversified investment portfolio that will reclaim your retirement, you should look at a three-pronged investment strategy: high-dividend stocks/ DRIPs, municipal bonds, and residential rental properties. You may want to start with stocks, and then, when enough money is coming in, add municipal bonds and, lastly, rental homes. Over time, you should strive for one-third stocks, one-third municipal bonds, and one-third real estate. This will give you a balanced portfolio that will generate cash every month for you.

You could put your money into CDs at the bank, but as of mid-2012, they were paying an interest rate of only 1–2 percent. Another more profitable avenue is to invest in stocks that pay high dividends, which are company stocks that pay a portion of their earnings each year as dividends to their stockholders.

If you choose this option, first open an online trading account with a company like E*Trade, TD Ameritrade, Scottrade, or ING Direct. This will allow you to pay discounted commissions whenever you buy or sell stocks. The fees range from $6 to $10 per trade. An online trading account also allows you to make the trades, buying or selling, whenever you want; you don't have to wait for a broker to execute the trades. "Resource Center, Item D" has a list of these discount brokers.

Once you have opened an account, you can deposit some money that you will use to buy high-dividend-paying stocks. "Resource Center, Item B" lists Bill Fisher's favorite stocks, including DRIPs.

Keep a couple of essential rules of investing in these stocks in mind. *First: Never — and I repeat, never — use margin to invest in stocks!* Margin is where a brokerage will advance you money to invest in stocks. It is essentially a high-interest loan that you have to pay back. If your stock's value crashes, the brokerage can immediately call in your loan to pay for the stock you bought. This is not fun, so don't ever buy stocks on margin.

Second: Don't take flyers that may tell an important and compelling story about unknown companies but that have little financial history and pay no dividends!

You should look at investing in stocks that are well-known names, that have positive earnings with a positive outlook, and that pay good dividends. *You should look at stocks that pay a dividend from between 2 and 5 percent!* This means that your stock will pay you 2–5 percent of the money you invested in the stock annually, for as long as the stock pays dividends.

It is important to note that companies can raise and lower their dividends whenever they decide, during their Board of Directors meeting, based upon their financial results each year. Therefore, it is good to look at a company's history of raising stock dividends over time. "Resource Center, Item H" lists companies that have raised their dividends each year for several consecutive years.

Another important rule is to avoid stocks that pay dividends that are too high! Stocks that pay over 6–7 percent may be subject to having their dividends cut, especially if their financials are not looking good for the future.

Another good rule of thumb is to look at a company's price to earnings (P/E) ratio. The P/E is the stock price divided by a company's earnings. In the middle of 2012, the average P/E ratio of all of the stocks in the stock market was around 19, meaning that if a stock had a P/E ratio of 19, it was fairly priced. Stocks above the 19 P/E are classified as too pricey, whereas stocks below the 19 P/E are inexpensive. *Therefore, an important rule is to select stocks that have a P/E ratio under 19!* These stocks have greater potential for appreciation or growth.

If you apply these rules to investing in high-dividend stocks, a recognized stock, such as ConocoPhillips, which has a P/E of 8.4 and pays a dividend of 3.5 percent, is an excellent investment target in the middle of 2012. Plus, knowing that ConocoPhillips has divided into two publically traded companies is only a bonus. If you held this stock at the time of the split, you would have received shares of the new company, which is Phillips 66, the refining portion of the company. Usually when a stock splits into two public companies, one of the stocks takes off and does better in appreciation. It is just another opportunity for growth in your nest egg. It can create greater shareholder value.

Another good rule is to diversify your stock holdings across different industries! As you are investing in stocks that pay high dividends, keep in mind that you should not put all of your money into stocks of one particular industry, such as retail stores. It is always a good practice to buy your stocks in different industries. If one industry gets hit by some bad news and all of your stocks were in that industry, you will take a financial hit across your entire stock portfolio. On the other hand, if you have a diversified portfolio of stocks, only one of two of your stocks will be hit and only a small percentage of your total stocks will go down. Some of the industries that you should consider investing in are petro-chemical, pharmaceutical, finance, banking, telecom, retail, mining, insurance, transportation, Internet, and high tech. Jim Cramer is an excellent resource to help you choose the right stocks. His website, www.thestreet.com, is a great place to examine all of his resources. He has written several books on investing, and he has a TV show called Mad Money on CNBC. You can also subscribe to his newsletter and email reports on investing.

Another good point to remember is that the whole world runs in cycles! Businesses have cycles. New businesses have a growth phase, a mature phase, and then a declining phase. If the business does not reinvent itself or come up with new products/services, it can eventually go out of business. The entire world economy runs in cycles. There are bull markets, where most of the stocks are going up and everything seems to be going great. There are also bear markets, where stocks continually go down and negativity reigns on Wall Street.

The point to realize is that you have to be flexible during these boom and bust times. You also have to be a bit of a contrarian. As stocks are rebounding and going up to their five-year highs, you should take a little off the table. You should sell a portion of your stocks to realize a profit in them. If stocks start retreating and going down, you should consider investing in the quality stocks that have five-year lows. Remember, you can look at the P/E ratio to judge the relative value of whether a stock is expensive, cheap, or fairly priced. A single-digit P/E typically indicates a good value for your money, and a P/E of over 20 generally indicates a stock is fairly valued and starting to get expensive.

The last thing you want to do during one of these market cycles is panic! Most people panic and sell when the market has fallen to its lowest level, and they typically buy when stocks are at their all-time highs. If you follow this philosophy, you will lose lots of money. You should not fall victim to this "knee jerk" reaction or the "follow the crowd" mentality.

If the market starts going down, don't panic and sell all of your stocks. You should hold onto the quality stocks that are paying the good dividends. It probably is a time to add to your positions. Conversely, if the market is going up continually, it is probably not a good time to pour more money into stocks. You should look at selling some of your stocks as they reach all-time highs.

As of mid-2012, dividends from stocks are taxed at a 15 percent rate annually, which may be a rate lower than your income tax rate. However, President Obama has proposed to raise the tax on dividends to your regular income tax rate. So if you are in the maximum tax category of 35 percent, you would have to pay 35 percent on your dividends from stocks. President Obama also is proposing to raise the maximum tax category from 35 percent to 39 percent. Regardless of what happens, high-dividend stocks are an excellent way to build back your nest egg.

DIVIDEND REINVESTMENT PROGRAMS (DRIPS)

Many public companies offer DRIP programs, where an individual can send in periodic checks to these companies to invest in their common stock directly, without going through a broker. The nice thing about these programs is that there are no broker fees associated with these DRIPs. Typically, there is a small fee to register and a small fee for each deposit into your account, but these fees are minimal and therefore small compared to what brokers charge.

First, you have to register with the company to participate in its DRIP program. Once registered, you can send in your checks, and the company will buy the stock and place it in your account. Each company will mail you a statement that shows your investment amount, how many shares you bought, and the new balance of your account. The company will also send you a statement when it pays out a dividend.

Another good reason to invest in DRIPs is that your dividends are automatically invested in more of that company's stock, and your account will grow every quarter, as long as the company is paying a dividend. You will get charged a very small trading fee on your statement each time the company buys more stock with your dividends, but the amount is tiny compared with what stockbrokers charge. Sometimes it is only a few pennies, and it depends upon how much money is being reinvested.

Bill Fisher was a huge DRIP investor, having over fifty DRIPs at the time of his passing. Bill was always good about sending in a spare $100 into his favorite DRIPs whenever he could.

One "must have" is the Chuck Carlson's DRIP Investor newsletter you can order for $74 per year. This guide lists all of the companies that offer a DRIP, their contact information, and what minimum initial amounts can be invested. You can either receive a hard copy or get the information online. The newsletter will also inform you of new companies that are initiating a DRIP program. A second DRIP newsletter is the *Buyers Guide to THE BEST DIVIDEND AND INCOME INVESTMENTS*, published by Horizon Publishing. This guide costs $39.97 per year. See "Resource Center, Item E" for details.

Remember that all of the rules that applied to investing in high-dividend stocks also apply to DRIP investing. *You want to look for quality stocks that pay a good dividend (2–5 percent), have an attractive P/E ratio (from 7 to 18), and are in diversified industries!*

MUNICIPAL BONDS

Another important piece of the three-pronged investment strategy is municipal bonds or "munis." With a municipal bond, you are lending your money to a city or local municipality to invest in specific projects within that locale. The bond money may be for a school district, a hospital, a toll road, or any of a number of projects for which a city needs money for financing. For the use of your money, the municipality pays you interest. Muni bonds are a very conservative investment. They are backed by the municipality that writes them and, let's face it, not many cities have gone bankrupt. I have been investing in muni bonds for almost thirty years, and I have never lost a penny. Bill Fisher invested in munis and never lost a penny.

Muni bonds are very boring. They are like watching paint dry or grass grow. These are investments that you buy and hold for the length of the bond, earning nice income every year. Muni bonds are not to be traded or speculated with. Even though there may be a time that the muni bond is worth more than you paid, you should not sell it because you would not be able to invest your new proceeds into another muni paying the same rate. Remember, we are in muni bonds for the income that it pays or accumulates. There will be more about this later.

There is a reason that brokers typically do not recommend muni bonds. Brokers are looking to make commissions through buying and selling of stocks and other investment products. These brokers will not make much money if you buy a muni bond from them and hold it for twenty years. That is why brokers are always recommending some hot speculative stock or a new Initial Public Offering (IPO) because they can make more money selling you this investment and then when you sell the investment, they make even more money.

There are two types of municipal bonds: coupon bonds and zeros. A coupon municipal bond is one that pays interest, usually twice each year, for the length of the bond. This is a good bond if you need the interest to live on or to invest elsewhere. Let's say that you bought a twenty-year muni bond at par with a 5 percent coupon with January and July payments for $100,000. This bond would pay you $2,500 in January and $2,500 in July, every year for twenty years. So you would be getting $5,000 each year for twenty years, or a total of $100,000 in interest over the twenty-year period. At the conclusion of the twenty years, you would get your original $100,000 investment back, thereby doubling your money.

The nice part of buying municipal bonds is that they are exempt from federal income taxes and depending upon which state you live in, they can be exempt from state income tax! With the example above, if you live in Texas, you would not pay any state or federal income taxes on any of the interest or the principal over the twenty-year investment. The higher the tax bracket you are in will result in the best benefits for tax-free bonds. If you are receiving a 5 percent return on your tax-free bonds and you are in the 33 percent income tax bracket, this is equivalent to a 7.46 percent taxable return. So keep this in mind if you are comparing investment alternatives.

The second type of municipal bond is a zero-coupon bond. This bond is also a loan from you to the municipality for a project, but this loan does not make interest payments to you each year. This bond pays all of the interest to you when the bond matures or the interest earned when you sell it. In the example above, this bond would pay you your principal and interest at the conclusion of the twenty-year period. It is also tax exempt, just like the coupon bond.

If you don't need the yearly income from the interest payments, this zero-coupon bond is good because you buy it at a much lower cost, and its payout can be substantial. An example of a zero-coupon municipal bond would be a $100,000 bond that matured in twenty years. In this example, you will have to invest only around $35,000 in the beginning, and the bond will grow in value over the twenty years until it matures and you receive the entire $100,000 — tax free. Zeros are actually good for younger individuals, like your children, because they have a long life ahead of them, and they can reap the full benefit of the zero by holding it until maturity.

Municipal bonds are tradable assets. You can buy and sell them every day the market is open. You could sell either one of the bonds in the examples above at any time during the twenty-year period. The amount you receive varies depending upon the interest rates and the price of the bonds at the time you sell them. If you have an interest rate of 5 percent on your muni and you sell it when interest rates climb to 6 percent, the value of your bond will be reduced by a small percentage because your 5 percent is not as competitive as the 6 percent rate now. If interest rates decline and you sell your 5 percent bond early, then you will make a small percentage on your investment because your 5 percent rate is more competitive than, let's say, 4 percent now. New buyers will be willing to pay you more for your bond to get the attractive 5 percent rate.

Instead of playing the market buying and selling muni bonds, I recommend you buy and hold the bonds to maturity! This way, you will receive all of the interest on your investment and you receive all of the original investment or principal back. You don't lose anything.

When investing in munis, you will find that interest rates fluctuate over time, so you want to be vigilant and wait for peaks in the bond interest rates. When inflation is roaring, you may find that muni bond rates can hit as high as 8 percent, or even higher. You want to be a buyer when this happens. When inflation is under control, bond rates can drop to 3 percent, which is not a good time to buy muni bonds. *I recommend buying munis when the rates hit 5 percent or more. I don't buy these bonds when they are under 5 percent!*

You will also find that terms for these bonds can vary from five years, ten years, fifteen years, twenty years, and even thirty years. Typically, the shorter-term bonds pay less interest than the longer-term bonds. The municipalities have to pay higher interest for the longer-term bonds to attract investors to tie up their money for such a long time. *It depends upon your situation, but I typically buy the long-term bonds for the higher returns!*

Municipal bonds are also rated for their credit worthiness and quality. They get grades of AAA, AA, A, BB, B, C, and any number of lower grades from rating agencies. A high grade, such as AAA, means that the bond is top quality and less likely to default. A grade below B is a low-quality grade, and bonds with these grades are not rated as favorable.

Low-grade muni bonds have to pay higher interest rates to attract investors, but the buyer needs to beware. *I recommend investing in muni bonds rated A or higher only!*

Some muni bonds also have insurance tied to them, which guarantees both the principal and interest. Because of the cost of the insurance, these bonds usually have a lower yield than the same bonds without the insurance. This is a coin toss. If you feel better with the insurance, then go ahead and purchase these bonds. It probably will help you sleep better at night. Alternatively, you can go without the insurance and get a higher yield. If you elect this option, I recommend picking bonds rated above A only. This option typically insures that you are picking the best-quality bonds available.

What about bond funds? Bond funds are a collection of muni bonds of varying quality. They typically have a floating interest rate based upon the makeup of the bonds invested. The bonds with the best quality get a lower interest rate, but they are more conservative and less likely to have a default. The worst-quality bond portfolios get a higher interest rate, but it becomes more likely that one of their bonds will default. I don't recommend buying bond funds. *I would buy only individual muni bonds!*

Another feature of a muni bond is that they can be either alternative minimum tax (AMT) or non-AMT. AMT means that the profits may be subject to the IRS alternative minimum tax each year. The rules are very complicated, and I recommend that if you purchase AMT bonds, you consult with your tax expert or accountant first. *As a rule, I never buy AMT muni bonds, nor would I recommend them!*

How do you buy muni bonds? You should contact the muni bond trader at your bank. This person sees all of the muni bonds that are available each day for investment. You can start by contacting your bank representative and get an introduction to the muni bond trader. When you are ready, tell the trader that you would be interested in buying a muni that trades at 5 percent or over at the investment level that you want. If bond rates are below 5 percent, then have the trader contact you when a bond that has a 5 percent coupon becomes available. Note that in most all cases, the sales commission on a muni bond is worked into the price already. There should not be a commission on top of what the bond costs. You can also buy munis through your discount brokerage or regular brokerage accounts.

RESIDENTIAL RENTAL PROPERTIES

After you have maxed out your IRA and your 401(k) and have started your high-dividend stock investments, DRIP investments and municipal bond investments, another investment opportunity and the third leg of the three-pronged investment strategy is to buy price depressed homes in nice neighborhoods with good schools and then rent them out to good families.

Many people have made and lost fortunes in real estate throughout the years. Real estate moves in cycles, and you can have boom and bust cycles. Residential real estate peaked in 2007 and went through a bust phase from 2008 to 2011. Many families lost their homes, and many homes are still sitting empty, having been foreclosed on by their lenders.

Now, over the next few years, 2012 through 2015, and maybe beyond, is a time to buy residential real estate and rent it. *The good thing about buying depressed residential real estate is that you can get a good return on your investment from rentals, plus you get the added bonus that the real estate could increase in value, as the market comes back!* As the economy gets better and more people are able to find jobs, they will want to either rent a nice home or buy one eventually. In any event, the values of the homes will start to increase again over the next few years.

Typically, you will have to put up a down payment for the property. This could run you 10–25 percent of the sale price. If you bought a $100,000 house, the down payment could run between $10,000 and $25,000. The rest of the purchase price can be financed with a mortgage over fifteen to thirty years. Mortgage rates in mid-2012 are at some of the lowest rates in history, so now is the time to lock in a low mortgage rate for your rental properties. If you have a good credit rating, you should be able to get a mortgage rate of 5–8 percent — and maybe lower — over the next few years.

In our example, if you bought a $100,000 house, put down $25,000, and financed the remainder of the money at 6 percent over thirty years, your house payment would be $553.83 per month. You should be able to rent your house from 7–10 percent of the purchase price per month, or $700 to $1,000 per month for the first twelve months. This example would make you a monthly profit of between $146 and $446 each month. You can then raise the rent by $50 to $100 per month every year, improving your return on investment each year.

Remember that you have to consider taxes, insurance, and repairs when calculating your total annual expenses. However, if you select the right property at the right price, you should be able to gain a net return of 7–10 percent each year on your investment. Also, remember that your house was bought at distressed prices, so its value should start appreciating over the next several years. A $100,000 house could gain as much as 50 percent over the next several years, reaping you, the buyer, a nice profit when you decide to sell.

Bill Fisher bought residential homes in Kansas City and rented them out to good families for several years in the 90s. When he sold them, he made profits in the range of 30–50 percent, plus he was able to make a solid return of 8–10 percent on the rentals each year.

Let me also tell you about one of my first residential home purchases that I made in 2005 (I still own the property), and review the numbers with you. My wife and I live in the Houston area, and in the summer of 2005, we purchased a three-bedroom, two-bath home with around 2,000 square feet of living space, which was to be a rental property. The home was in a neighborhood zoned to Bellaire High School, a good high school in the Houston Independent School District. We were inexperienced in rental investing at the time and made a lot of mistakes in the beginning, paying too much for the property and spending too much on remodeling. However, over the course of the last seven years, our investment has turned significantly in our favor.

We paid $305,000 for this house, which at the time was a fully priced house. This was not a depressed price since the recession of 2008 had not hit yet. We put about $40,000 into the house, which included new paint, landscaping, and refurbishing the swimming pool. We rented the house, initially for $3,400 per month, which was a net gain of $820 per month. After two years, we raised the rent to $3,600 for two more years, now increasing the net to $1,020 per month. We have a good renter, who is never late and very rarely calls about repairs.

The value of the house during this time rose from $305,000 to a high of $430,000 during the peak of 2007. It then retreated back to around $375,000 during the middle of 2012. The value is currently starting to rebound and move back up again. Housing prices in Houston did not drop as much as in other areas in the country, and the foreclosure rate in Texas has been very low.

In analyzing this rental purchase, we paid $305,000 for the property and have received $168,000 in rental payments over four years. If we continue to rent the property for four more years at the same rate, we will have received a total eight-year rental amount of $336,000, which is over the original purchase price of the house and close to the purchase price of the house when you consider the $40,000 in improvements. During the time we have owned the house, we have been able to pay off the fifteen-year mortgage with advance payments. The beauty of this scenario is that we now have a paid-off rental house that is paying us a great return, and its value is appreciating.

Not every housing market in the country is as good as the Texas market. California, Arizona, Nevada, Michigan, and Florida have had severe price reductions and large numbers of foreclosures in the recent recession, which can be good for negotiating low purchase prices, but you may have a difficult time finding renters for your property. When you investigate the rental market in your area, be sure to look at how many homes are being advertised as rentals. Also, look at what rents are in your area so that you can work your numbers to see if a rental property investment in your area makes sense.

Another factor you will want to look at is whether any corporations are planning to move into your area! These moves typically are announced in your local newspaper or on the local television news. If a company is planning to build a new office in your area and is hiring one thousand new workers, this would be a good opportunity to acquire rental properties near the new company location.

You also want to make sure that your potential rental property is located in a good school district! Families with school-aged children want to be in homes with good schools. Again, I am very familiar with the Texas real estate market. Some of the better schools in the Houston area are The Woodlands, Klein, Kingwood, Sugarland, Katy, Memorial, Stratford, and Bellaire. You will have to check out the elementary, middle schools, and high schools in the areas that you are researching. "Resource Center, Item I" lists some of the better school districts in the Texas area.

Another important factor to consider when reviewing potential rental acquisitions is the age of the house. *It is typically better to buy a rental property that was built in the last seven years, or since 2005!* These newer homes are usually built with better construction materials, are more modern, have energy-efficient features such as radiant barrier and extra insulation, and have energy-efficient appliances. These newer features will save dramatically on energy bills, which will be a great attraction for families looking to rent.

In addition, an older property built in the 60s or 70s could require some serious, costly repairs. You should be able to discover these problems when you do your inspections, and you can use these problems to bargain down the purchase price or require that they be remedied. However, what if you purchase one of these older homes and the plumbing or electrical wiring just wears out after forty years of use? You could be looking at spending a good sum of money.

Again, I am familiar with the Texas residential markets, and Houston, Dallas, Austin, and San Antonio are good markets to acquire inexpensive housing for rental properties. The rental rates have been going up over the last several months, and rental homes are being sought after as a nicer lifestyle than apartments. Corporations are also planning new offices in Texas. For example, Exxon is building a new national headquarters in northwest Houston in the Spring area, and ConocoPhillips is planning new offices in the Beltway 8/

Interstate 10 area, which would bring new rental demand to the Stratford and Memorial areas. "Resource Center, Item G" lists the better communities in the Texas area for acquiring home rentals, and "Resource Center, Item L" includes a partial list of real estate agents in the four major metropolitan areas of Texas.

When you're evaluating the purchase of a new rental property, one good measure for you to use is the home's cost per square foot. In different subdivisions of a city, the cost per square foot can vary considerably. If you examine an expensive subdivision, the price per square foot can run over $200. In less expensive neighborhoods, the price per square foot can run in the $100 range. In some of the outlying areas of cities in Texas, the price per square foot can run as low as $50. You can use this measure to evaluate the value of each house as compared to other houses. It would be almost impossible to build a new home at $50 per square foot, for example.

Another great resource that will help you find residential homes in the United States is www.zillow.com, which allows you to search specific subdivisions in selected cities for homes that are for sale. You can search by dollar amount, square footage of the home, lot size, number of bedrooms, and other categories. Zillow also lists foreclosures and short sales that are available in your selected areas. Your local real estate association should have an interactive website that you can use to locate residential properties and also tell you what rents are going for in your area.

The Eagle Ford Shale area below San Antonio, Texas, will be an interesting opportunity for rental properties over the next several years. This very rural area of southern Texas has tremendous deposits of oil shale under the ground. With a new technique called "hydraulic fracturing," petroleum companies shoot water down into these subterranean structures, allowing them to extract the oil from the ground at a very productive rate. With oil staying around $100 per barrel, oil companies can make good money drilling in this area and, consequently, many oil companies are pouring more and more resources into the area to find new oil deposits. North Dakota and Pennsylvania have similar oil shale areas.

Along with this increased drilling activity comes an influx of new workers to a very rural area that has no housing for these extra workers. Some workers are forced to commute two hours to and from work because there is no available housing. Entrepreneurs are buying up land and building "man camps," apartments, hotels, and RV parks. The oil companies are paying high rents to house their men, sometimes as high as $100 per night per person, and they are pre-paying for up to two years for the properties. See "Resource Center, Item J" for more information on opportunities in the Eagle Ford Shale area.

Another question to ponder when considering purchasing residential real estate is this" "How do I manage my properties, especially when I am located in another state?" You can do it yourself, having the renters make out the checks to you each month. You can also find contractors, such as repairmen, electricians, landscape services, and air conditioning companies to maintain your home or work on it when it has problems.

Another way to manage these remote properties is through a real estate management company near your properties. A management company can collect your rents for you and maintain your home through a network of vendors that work for that company. If you select this option, interview these companies and make sure they are trustworthy and easy to work with. "Resource Center, Item K" contains a list of property management companies and real estate agents in Texas.

One last item to consider when renting your newly acquired home is who you will select to be the renter. When you purchase the home and put it on the market for rent, you will receive applications or contracts from prospective renters. You should be happy that you are receiving applications, but you don't want to just take the first renter that shows up.

When selecting your renter, be sure and ask for employment records and a credit report on all of the parties (husband and wife) that will be living in the home. After you receive this information, review it carefully. You should make sure that the potential renters have a good credit history; one that does not have late payments or unpaid outstanding balances. You should also examine the total income of the renters to insure that they will have enough income to cover your rent plus their other expenses. *I like to see a figure of at least three times the rent in their monthly income.*

A review of their employment history is good to give you an indication of how long the renters stay at different companies. If you see a lot of moving around and short duration jobs, then you might have a problem with rental payments, if they lose or change jobs.

Of course, you can't discriminate against potential renters for race, color or creed, but you can make a decision on who you think the best renter will be based upon financial considerations.

THE BEAUTY OF COMPOUND INTEREST

Compound interest, where you allow the interest from your investments to be reinvested continually over the course of several years, is a beautiful concept. When you do this, it is amazing how much money you can earn.

Let's say you have a $100,000 investment opportunity that pays 5 percent over a thirty-year period. If you refrained from taking out any money or interest and let the interest be plowed back into the principal, the principal would grow and the interest would increase whenever more interest was plowed back into the principal. It becomes a snowball effect, where a snowball is rolled downhill, and as the snowball goes downhill, it picks up more snow and becomes larger and larger until it gets to the bottom of the hill and has become a boulder of snow.

In the above example, at the end of ten years, your initial $100,000 would be worth $162,889.46. At the end of twenty years, your money would have grown to $265,329.77. At the end of thirty years, your original $100,000 would be up to

$432,194.24. It is truly amazing that your investment would have almost tripled your money.

Keep this concept in mind when you have extra money to invest. *Compound interest will grow your money faster if you allow the interest to be reinvested year after year!*

CONCLUSION

The 2008–2010 recession was brutal, eliminating as much as 50 percent of Baby Boomers' retirement nest eggs. Many Boomers were stunned, were frightened, and did not know how to recover from this catastrophic loss. Many were forced to go back to work just to make ends meet.

Now that we are coming out of these bad economic times, Boomers need to reexamine their financial positions and develop a solid plan on how to proceed over the next several years. Let's face it; when individuals turn sixty-five, they are not old or obsolete. If you have your health, you may live another thirty years. That is a long time. Therefore, you must ensure you have a plan that will generate new income so that you can live a nice lifestyle and have money left over to invest.

Every time you think you want to give up and sit on the couch and watch the world go by, remember or reread *The Boomer's Guide to Recovering Your Lost Retirement*. At seventy-two years old, Bill started from scratch investing in stocks that paid high dividends as well as DRIPs, municipal bonds, and residential real estate. Bill continued to work in the telecom industry and invested his Social Security and pension money. Bill lived a great life, traveled abroad, and still succeeded in amassing a $1 million investment portfolio over the course of sixteen years.

You can do the same! I wish you and your family health, wealth, and wisdom. Go forth and conquer!

RESOURCE CENTER

A. AGENT INFORMATION

Here is a list of agent opportunities for Boomers:

> A+ Conferencing—I founded this conference-calling company in 2000. It sells audio, web, and desktop video conferencing services to businesses and nonprofit organizations. A+ markets its services exclusively through agents and resellers. Currently, A+ has about three hundred registered agents and fifteen resellers. Most of these agents work out of their homes and use the telephone to call businesses in their area in order to save them money on their conference-calling services. Some of these agents make over six-figure incomes selling these services. For more information, go to www.aplusconferencing.com, or call Mary Hawkins at 888-239-3969.

> AireSpring—This telecom company offers an array of business telecom services, including long distance, virtual PBX, cloud services, and data networking. You can get more

information by visiting www.airespring.com and clicking on the Agent tab, or you can call 866-925-9803, #391.

> CenturyLink—This telecom company offers a multitude of business telecom services, including long distance, local service, virtual PBX, cloud services, and data networking. You can get more information by visiting www.centurylink.com/business or by calling 800-366-8201.

> Level 3—This global company provides virtually every telecom service, including Internet access, local service, long distance, virtual PBX, data networking, and cloud services. You can get more information by visiting www.level3.com and clicking on the Partner Program or by calling 877-253-8353.

> Liberty Power Corp.—This electricity reseller targets small to medium-sized businesses. It currently provides electricity to California, Texas, Illinois, Pennsylvania, New York, Maine, Massachusetts, Rhode Island, Connecticut, New Jersey, and Maryland. To get more information about becoming an agent, you can contact Guy Southeaver at 954-958-5311 or gsoutheaver@libertypowercorp.com.

> Telarus—This telecom company offers an array of telecom services, including Internet access, local service, and long distance service. You can reach Telarus by visiting www.telarus.com or by calling 877-346-3232.

> World Telecom Group—WTG is a telecom company that offers services from a group of specialized providers in every aspect of telecom services. You can find out more information by visiting www.worldtelecomgroup.com or by calling 310-456-2200.

> If you are considering becoming a telecom agent, you should visit the Channel Partners website at www.channelpartnersonline.com. This group publishes the *Channel Partners* magazine and hosts a semiannual trade show targeted at agents working in the telecom industry.

B. BILL FISHER'S FAVORITE STOCKS

Below is the list of stocks that Bill Fisher invested in directly and through DRIPs:

AT&T (T)

Aqua America (WTR)

Caterpillar (CAT)

Colgate Palmolive (CL)

CSX Corporation (CSX)

Dominion Resources (D)

Empire District Electric
Co. (EDE)

Garmin (GRMN)

Halliburton (HAL)

Intel (INTC)

KC Southern (KSU)

Laclede Group (LG)

McDonald's (MCD)

Phillip Morris (PM)

Proctor & Gamble (PG)

Southern Union Co. (SUG)

Sprint (S)

Walgreens (WAG)

Anadarko (APC)

Baxter (BAX)

Coca-Cola (KO)

ConocoPhillips (COP)

Daimler Chrysler (DDAIF)

Eli Lilly (LLY)

ExxonMobil (XOM)

General Mills (GIS)

Hugoton Royalty (HGT)

Johnson & Johnson (JNJ)

Kraft (KFT)

Merck (MRK)

Monsanto (MON)

Piedmont Natural Gas (PNY)

Southern Company (SO)

Spectra Energy (SE)

Verizon (VZ)

Yum Brands (YUM)

C. DAVE RAMSEY'S INFORMATION

www.DaveRamsey.com
D. Discount Broker Websites
www.etrade.com
www.Interactivebrokers.com   www.schwab.com
www.scottrade.com   www.sharebuilder.com
www.tdameritrade.com
E. DRIP Information
Buyers Guide to the Best Dividend and Income Investments —
http://www.horizonpublishing.com/Images/
Sample_2008_1_Income_Book.pdf; 800-233-5922.
Chuck Carlson DRIP newsletter — www.dripinvestor.com;
800-233-5922.
F. IRS Government Website
www.irs.gov/retirement/index.html

G. LIST OF COMMUNITIES IN THE FOUR MAJOR TOWNS IN TEXAS FOR RENTAL HOMES

Austin

Bastrop
Brushy Creek
Del Valle
Eubank Acres
Hays
Lake Travis
Lost Creek
Manor
Northwest Hills
Pflugerville
Round Rock
Spicewood
Wells Branch

Buda
Cedar Park
Dripping Springs
Georgetown
Kyle
Leander
Manchaca
McNeill
Oak Hill
Pleasant Hill
Shady Hollow
Vinson

Dallas

Addison
Arlington
Carrollton
Coppell
Farmers Branch
Garland
Grapevine
Hurst
Keller
Lewisville
Oaktree
Preston Trails
Southlake Carroll
University Park

Allen
Briar Ridge Estates
Colleyville
Duncanville
Flower Mound
Grand Prairie
Highland Village
Irving
Lancaster
McKinney
Plano
Richardson
Southwest Frisco
White Rock Lake

Houston
Bellaire
Fulshear
Jersey Village
Kingwood
Meyerland
Spring
Sugarland
The Woodlands

Clear Lake City
Humble
Katy
Memorial West
Oak Forest
Spring Valley
The Heights

San Antonio
Alamo Heights
Boerne
Bulverde
Cibolo
Heafner
Kentwood Manor
North Loop
Palo Alto Heights
Saint Hedwig
Shavano Park
Terrell Hills
Wetmore

Balcones Heights
Buena Vista
Castle Hills
Columbia Heights
Hollywood Park
Leon Valley
Olmos Park
Phoenix
Schertz
Stone Oak
The Dominion
Windcrest

H. LIST OF COMPANIES THAT HAVE RAISED DIVIDENDS FOR TWENTY CONSECUTIVE YEARS OR MORE

For a complete list of these companies, go to www.the-dynamicdividend.com.

Diebold Inc. (DBD)	58 years
American States Water Company (AMR)	57 years
Dover Corporation (DOV)	56 years
Northwest Natural Gas (NWN)	56 years
Emerson Electric (EMR)	55 years
Genuine Parts Co. (GPC)	55 years
Procter & Gamble Co. (PG)	55 years
3M Co. (MMM)	53 years
Vectren Corp. (VVC)	52 years
Cincinnati Financial Corp (CINF)	50 years
Johnson & Johnson (JNJ)	49 years
Coca-Cola Co. (KO)	49 years
Leggett & Platt (LEG)	40 years
Abbott Labs (ABT)	39 years
Kimberly Clark (KMB)	39 years
Pepsico, Inc. (PEP)	39 years
McGraw-Hill (MHP)	38 years
Automatic Data Processing (ADP)	36 years
McDonald's Corp (MCD)	35 years
Pitney-Bowes (PBI)	29 years
ExxonMobil (XOM)	29 years
AT&T (T)	27 years
PPG Industries (PPG)	26 years
Chevron Corp (CVX)	24 years
General Dynamics (GD)	20 years

I. LIST OF GOOD SCHOOL DISTRICTS IN THE FOUR MAJOR METROPOLITAN AREAS IN TEXAS

For a complete list of school districts, go to www.greatschools. org.

Austin

Austin ISD	Bastrop ISD
Del Valle ISD	Dripping Springs ISD
Eanes ISD	Georgetown ISD
Hays ISD	Lake Travis ISD
Leander ISD	Manor ISD
Pflugerville ISD	Round Rock ISD

Dallas

Allen ISD	Argyle ISD
Arlington ISD	Carroll ISD
Carrollton-Farmers Branch ISD	Coppell ISD
Dallas ISD	Denton ISD
Ft. Worth ISD	Frisco ISD
Garland ISD	Granbury ISD
Grand Prairie ISD	Grapevine-Colleyville ISD
Highland Park ISD	Hurst-Euless-Bedford ISD
Keller ISD	Lewisville ISD
Northwest ISD	Plano ISD

Houston

Conroe ISD	Cypress Fairbanks ISD
Fort Bend ISD	Houston ISD
Humble ISD	Katy ISD
Klein ISD	North Forest ISD
Pearland ISD	Spring Branch ISD

San Antonio

Alamo Heights ISD	Boerne ISD

Edgewood ISD

Judson ISD

Northeast ISD

Northside ISD

Schertz-Cibolo ISD

J. OPPORTUNITIES IN THE EAGLE FORD SHALE AREA

http://www.energyandcapital.com/articles/
the-eagle-ford-shale-formation/1820
http://petrochase.com/blog/?tag=eagle-ford-shale
http://shale.typepad.com/eaglefordshale/
http://www.southtexasranches.com/Track-Eagle-Ford-
Shale-Real-Estate-For-Sale.html
http://www.eaglefordshale.com/
http://www.dockery.cc/

K. PARTIAL LIST OF PROPERTY MANAGEMENT COMPANIES IN TEXAS

Austin

1. www.americasdiscountrealty.com   888-990-7653
   billburnsre@yahoo.com   512-358-1191
2. www.amgaustin.com   512-310-9015
3. www.austinpropertymanagement.com 512-342-9566
4. www.atxmanagement.com   512-990-3551
   Jessica@atxmanagement.com
5. www.pioneeraustin.com   512-310-9015
   info@pioneeraustin.com

Dallas

1. www.cwsparks.com   214-948-3192
2. www.onepropdfw.com   800-841-9299
   kGillespie@oneprop.com
3. www.powerproperties.com   214-550-0000
   Jason@powerproperties.com
4. www.propertymanagementdallas.net   214-534-8980
5. www.victorypark.com   214-303-5535
   katiehoward@cousinsproperties.com

Houston

1. www.houston4lease.com   800-571-5212
2. www.houstonpropertymanagementtx.com
                                          832-585-8004

3. www.memorialpropertymanagement.com
                                          866-567-7364
                                          713-973-1001
4. www.terraresidential.com   800-275-7776
   jsteward@terraresidential.com   713-895-9966
5. www.txhomesrealty.com   281-646-9929
   info@txhomesrealty.com

San Antonio

1. www.davidsonproperties.com   210-826-1616
   mail@dpisat.com
2. www.homelocatorsrealty.com   888-374-4600
3. www.libertymgt.net   800-732-4276
                                        210-681-8080
4. www.sanantoniopropertymanagement.com
                                        210-658-0928

   richard.prater@rea.com
5. www.sa-nwrealestate.com   210-521-7900
   nwre@swbell.com

L. PARTIAL LIST OF REAL ESTATE AGENTS IN TEXAS

Austin

1. www.americasdiscountrealty.com   888-990-7653
   billburnsre@yahoo.com   512-358-1191
2. www.austintexashomes.com   512-796-7653
3. www.realtyaustin.com   888-287-7356
   realtor@realtyaustin.com   512-328-8000
4. www.strubresidential.com   512-524-5558
   mark@strubresidential.com
5. www.uptownrealtyaustin.com   512-651-0505

Dallas

1. www.dallas-realtor.net   972-591-3560
2. www.dfwrealestate.com   214-637-6660
3. www.ebby.com   214-303-1133
   eresource@ebby.com
4. www.kw.com   972-599-7000
5. www.virginiacook.com   214-750-7373
   plano@virginiacook.com

Houston

1. www.garygreene.com   800-231-0707
   realestateservices@garygreene.com
2. www.johndaugherty.com   281-685-4402
   Raybon@johndaugherty.com
3. www.marthaturner.com   888-520-1981
      713-520-1981
4. www.OasisRealtyTeam.com   281-221-2276
   Patty@OasisRealtyTeam.com
5. www.westsiderealtors.com   281-925-3000

San Antonio

1. www.angelodavisrealtor.com   210-408-2500
   adavis@cbharper.com

2. www.gosahome.com   210-493-3030
3. www.kingrealtors.com   800-828-5560
   homes@kingrealtors.com   210-826-2345
4. www.satxproperty.com   210-319-4960
   randy@satxproperty.com
5. www.zarsandrogers.com   210-209-8711

M. SAMPLE AGENT AGREEMENT FOR A+ CONFERENCING
A+ CONFERENCING (A+)
MASTER AGENT AGREEMENT

This agreement is between A+ Conferencing (A+) and _____ (client). The purpose of this agreement is for A+ to provide conference calling and teleservices to customers of client for just consideration from these clients; and A+ will pay client a commission on all of clients' customers paid invoices. This agreement will be in effect for a period of five years, and at the conclusion of the five-year period it will continue in effect on a month-to-month basis, until the agreement is terminated in writing by either party.

A+ agrees to:

1. Provide conference calling and teleservices to client and its customers.
2. Set up all accounts, issue pin codes, handle all calls, and bill the respective customers directly.
3. Bill the clients' customers at the client's suggested rates.
4. Give the client a buy rate of 1 cpm for Local Meet Me and 2.9 cpm for 800 Meet Me for reservationless calling, and 8 cpm for op assist lite, 10 cpm for Op assist Toll Meet me and 12 cpm for Op assist, 800 Meet Me and 12 cpm for Dial Out for operator assisted calling. Web conferencing is: StartWebShare, .03 cpm; Multi Media StartVisuals (IBM), .08 cpm; and WebEx, .21 cpm. Should any vendor raise its price to A+, A+ will give client 30-day advance notice of any increase.
5. Handle all customer service and complaints from clients' customers.

6. Pay commissions to client on a twice per month basis.

7. Keep client's list of customers confidential and not use it in any way without the express approval from the client.

8. For large volume customers, negotiate rates and commissions on a case-by-case basis.

9. For toll flat rate, unlimited, 24/7 traffic, give the client the buy rates provided on the attached sheet, schedule A. Flat rate service is not guaranteed and is dependent upon port capacity.

10. On all large volume, per minute accounts, discounted rates may be available and A+ will pay client a minimum of 10 percent of all gross revenue, regardless of sell price. A+ will pay 10 percent on all revenue brought by sub-agents, agents, or resellers recruited by master agent. A+ will pay 10 percent on all conference bridge sales, leases, or maintenance contracts.

Client agrees to:

1. Utilize A+ as client's conference calling and teleservices vendor on a non-exclusive basis.

2. Be classified as an independent contractor for this agreement and as such responsible for your own taxes.

3. Not be employed simultaneously by a conference calling competitor.

4. Assist in promoting conference calling and teleservices to commercial and nonprofit organizations.

Both parties agree to defend and hold harmless the other against all claims by any third parties arising out of or related to the actions or omissions of the indemnifying parties in connection with its obligations under this agreement.

Both parties agree to keep the other's information and client information confidential and to not disclose this information or the contents of this agreement without the other's consent.

Either party may cancel this agreement for any reason with written notice to the other party. Commissions on agent accounts will continue to be paid to agents that continue to do business with A+.

Rates are subject to change with a 30-day written notice to client.

A+ Conferencing may, for operational reasons, change the codes or numbers utilized by A+ to provide the Service or vary the technical specifications of the Service, provided any change to the technical specification does not materially affect the performance of the Service.

NON CIRCUMVENTION: Both parties agree that no effort shall be made to circumvent either party in an attempt to gain commission, fees, remunerations, or considerations to the benefit of any of the signatories of this Agreement, while excluding equal or agreed to benefit any of the other signatories. Non-circumvention agreement will be in force for the duration of this agreement and for a period of at least two (2) years after the termination date of the agreement. Both parties also agree to not recruit each other's employees, agents, or resellers without the consent of the other party.

VENUE: This agreement shall be governed by the laws of the State of Texas. Venue for any action related to this contract shall be in Houston, Texas.

ENTIRE AGREEMENT: This agreement represents the entire agreement of the parties with respect to the subject matter hereof and supersedes all prior oral or written agreements. This agreement may be modified only in writing, signed by both parties.

FORCE MAJEURE: The parties' performance under this agreement shall be excused if such nonperformance is due to labor difficulties, governmental orders, civil commotions, acts of nature, adverse weather conditions, and other circumstances beyond the parties' control.

SIGNED AND ACCEPTED: SIGNED AND ACCEPTED:

A+ CONFERENCING

Signature	Signature
Printed Name	Printed Name
Title	Title
	Address
	City, State, Zip
	Telephone Fax Email

SCHEDULE A
MASTER AGENT WHOLESALE BUY RATES

Wholesale Buy Rates	Suggested Retail Rates

Per Minute Audio

Automated Reservationless
Toll Meet Me/Local Dial In =
.01 cents/line/minute   .03–.05 cents/line/minute
Toll Meet Me =
.01 cents/line/minute   .04–.06 cents/line/minute
800 Meet Me (Interstate domestic)
= .029 cents/line/minute   .05–.07 cents/line/minute
800 Meet Me (Canada) =
.039 cents/line/minute   .06–.08 cents/line/minute
International Toll Free Service available from selected countries; call for quote.

Operator Assisted
Toll Meet Me =
.08 cents/line/minute   .15–.22 cents/line/minute
800 Meet Me – Lite =
.10 cents/line/minute   .09–.14 cents/line/minute
800 Meet Me (domestic)
= .12 cents/line/minute   .19–.25 cents/line/minute
Domestic Op Dial Out
= .12 cents/line/minute   .19–.25 cents/line/minute
International Op Dial Out rates vary by country and can be sent upon request.

Flat Rate Toll Audio
7/24 Unlimited Usage/50 parties
= $25/month $ 75–$150/month
7/24 Unlimited Usage/20 parties
= $10/month $ 40–$ 80/month
7/24 Unlimited Usage/10 parties
= $5/month $ 20–$ 60/month
Flat Rate–Extra Parties
= $0.50 per line/mo $2.00–$3.00 per line/
                                         month
Plans for 350+ are priced at $1.50 per line/month
                             $2.00–$3.00 per line/month
Flat Rate Call Detail = $25/month/set of pins
                             $35/month/set of pins
(Call detail fee will not apply for resellers.)

Flat Rate Web Conferencing, Multi Media StartVisuals
(includes toll audio) (IBM Product)
24/7 Unlimited Usage/100 parties
= $220/month $300–$500/month
24/7 Unlimited Usage/50 parties
= $120/month $170–$250/month
24/7 Unlimited Usage/20 parties
= $60/month $100–$175/month
24/7 Unlimited Usage/10 parties
= $40/month $70–$120/month
24/7 Unlimited Usage/5 parties
= $30/month $60–$100/month

Flat Rate Desktop Video, Start-Video.com (True toll audio
included, VOIP audio available)
24/7 Unlimited Usage
$2 per party per month $4–$5 per party per month

**Please note: All flat rate products require pre-payment by customer if A+ is doing the billing.

Ancillary Services
Billing = $3.50 per bill   (resellers only)   Not Apply
Operator Q&A
= 0.03 cents per minute (+op assist rate)   0.05 cents per minute (+op assist rate)
Operator Polling = same as Q&A   same as Q&A

Operator Com Line = $50/hour-rounded to next hour $60-75/hour

Operator Monitor
= $50/hour, rounded to next hour
                                    $60/hour, rounded to next hour
Operator Record (auto calls only)
= $25/recording $35-50 per recording
        No extra charge for op to record on op assist calls
Automated Q&A
= $50/hour, rounded to next hour $60-75/hour
Sub Conferencing
= No Charge (only per min rate)   No Charge (only per min rate)

Participant List
= $1 per name, Maximum $50 $1.50 per name, Maximum $75

Overbooking Fee =$2 per port, if over 80 percent does not show on reserved calls
Transcription Services
= $45 per transcription hr. $50-$75 per transcription hr.
Reminder Calls = $1 per call $2 per call

CD = $20 per CD, plus shipping $25–$40 per CD, plus shipping

FTP = $15 $20–$35 per file

****

Web Conferencing allows you to view slides, chat, share documents, take web tours, and collaborate on documents.

Per Minute Web Conferencing
StartWebShare = .03 cents per minute .05–.08 cents per minute
StartVisuals = .08 cents per minute   .12–.18 cents per minute
WebEx = .21 cents per minute   .25–.35 cents per minute

Web Casting (Streaming) allows you to stream your conference call over a website and participants can listen to the call via their PC and the Internet. In addition, you can upload your slides to us and we can put your slides on a web page, allowing conference call participants to listen to the call over the telephone connection and view the slides over the Internet as they are being discussed. We use push technology to advance the slides at the appropriate times in the presentations.

Flat Rate Web Casting (Streaming):
Web casting* = $600 per call $750 per call
Web casting with slides* = $700 per 90 min call $850 per call
Note: All Web casting is flat rate, regardless of number of participants. There are no set up fees or uploading of slides fees.

****

Flat Rate Voicemail Service: (Unified Messaging)
Includes Turnkey Private Label Website at No Additional Charge!
Voice Mail Service
= $24.95 per month $34.95 per month or higher
        + one time activation fee of $15 + one time activation fee of $15

Digital Podium Replay Service:

Basic Service – Includes unlimited 24/7 replay on toll dial in number, Digital Podium online account
If purchased as standalone product:
Wholesale cost: $50/month   Retail cost: $99/month
If purchased with a flat rate account:
Wholesale cost: $35/month   Retail cost: $65/month

Premium Service - Includes basic replay features plus unlimited FTP downloads at no additional charge
Wholesale cost: $100/month Retail cost: $199/month

Premium Plus Web – Includes premium service features plus unlimited web archiving.
Wholesale cost: $200/month   Retail cost: $300/month

Audio Archiving with Web Streaming – Our operators dial in and capture recording of your conference call. Audio Archive is posted on the Digital Podium replay site for 30 days. Option to collect registration data from listeners, can include name, company, email, etc. Includes unlimited replay on toll dial in number (optional).
Wholesale cost: $125/month   Retail cost: $250/month

Proclaim Video Email Service

This service is an excellent prospecting tool for new business. Instead of receiving a cold text e-mail, your prospects can see you in full motion video, delivering your message and using PowerPoint presentations to illustrate your main points. Proclaim lets you easily create recorded video messages that are available on demand or hold live meetings with a single click.
Proclaim stores a library of video / audio content and PowerPoint slides to roll in at any time to complement the presentation. You call on just the right media pieces from your playlist to add substance and style to each personalized video meeting or message that you do.

Features	QuickTouch	Advanced	Deluxe
Total Viewing Minutes / Month	2,000	2,000	5,000
Record Message Capability	yes	yes	yes
Live Meeting Capability	no	yes	yes
Live Participants / Meeting	N/A	25	50
Upload Content Capability	PPTs /video	PPTs /video	PPTs /video
Send Email Capability	yes	yes	yes
Playlist	yes	yes	yes
Statistics	yes	yes	yes
Registration	yes	yes	yes
Branding	yes	yes	yes
Email "Message Watched" Notification	no	no	yes
Message Producer	no	no	yes
Blog Posting	no	no	yes
Support Available	Web	Web / Phone	Web /Phone
Storage (stored documents	--	5 GB	10 GB
Message Branding is available for an additional one-time fee of $100			

Proclaim Service Level	Wholesale Buy Rate	Suggested Retail
QuikTouch	$19/mth. Overage .04 CPM	$39–$49/mth.
Advanced (Per Minute)	.05	.07–.09
Advanced	$37/mth. Overage .04 CPM	$49–$99/mth.
Deluxe	$74/mth. Overage .04 CPM	$99–$149/mth.
White Label Branding	$350	$500

Large Account Processing (Proclaim Deluxe)		
25,000 min month	$1000 commitment	$.04 per minute overage
50,000 min month	$1500 commitment	$.03 per minute overage
100,000 min month	$2000 commitment	$.02 per minute overage

Questions? Please contact Mary at 888-239-3969 or maryh@nwpros.com.

*Larger accounts will be handled on a case-by-case basis. Agents make 20 percent commission on all large account sales.

N. SAMPLE TELEMARKETING SCRIPT WITH REBUTTALS
Telemarketing Script – Conference Calling Services
A+ CONFERENCING
TELEMARKETING SCRIPT

May I please speak with the person that handles your conference calling? What is that person's name, please? Thank you.

Hello, my name is _____, calling from A+ Conferencing. How are you today? That's good.

I'm calling to see if you do any conference calling there and to see if we can get you a better rate. Let me ask you a couple of questions:

1. How much conferencing do you do each month?
2. Are you using reservationless conferencing?
3. How much are you paying per minute?
4. Which vendor are you currently using?

IF PROSPECT IS INTERESTED, THEN YOU CAN SELL THE SERVICE AT 1 CENT UNDER THE PROSPECT'S CURRENT PRICING (IF PROSPECT WILL NOT TELL YOU THE RATE, THEN START OFF WITH 1.5 CENTS FOR 713 MEET ME SERVICE AND 3.9 CENTS FOR 800 MEET ME SERVICE).

Mr(s)._____, we can give you a rate of _____ cents per minute, which will save you substantially over what you have now. To get started, I just need to fax you our half-page application. Just fill it out and fax it back to me at 713-780-5931. When I get that back, we will call you with your telephone number (or 800 number) and your pin codes and you will be ready to start conferencing immediately. Would that be okay?

IF NO OR DON'T WANT TO CHANGE: I certainly understand. What I would like to do is offer you a free call. We will give you a 713 telephone number and set of pin codes for you to try our service and see the quality of the connections. Would that be okay?

IF STILL NO: Thank you for speaking with me. Have a good day!

QUESTIONS & REBUTTALS

What types of conferencing do you provide? We specialize in the following:

1. 713 Meet Me, reservationless calls – This type of conference is where all the parties call into a 713 telephone number, input their seven-digit pin code followed by the # sign when prompted by the attendant, and then they are in the conference. They can talk as long as they desire and they can place conferences twenty-four hours a day, seven days a week, without ever having to make a reservation.

   800 Meet Me, reservationless calls – This type of conference is the same as above except all the parties dial an 800 number to access the bridge. All of the other procedures are identical.

   Operator Assisted Conferencing – This type of conferencing requires an operator to answer or complete your calls for you and therefore requires higher pricing (10 cents more per minute).

2. I have a contract with another vendor (MCI, AT&T, PGI, Intercall, etc.). I understand. Conference calling typically falls outside of their contracts, and they don't know that you are dialing another 800 number to do conference calls. Plus, think of the savings you will have with the lower rate. Can I fax or email you an application?

3. Are there any contracts? No. All you have to do to get started is to fill out the half-page application and fax it back to me. We will then call you back with a telephone number (800 number) and your set of pin codes and you are ready to start calling immediately.

4. Why do you need two pin codes? One pin code is for the moderator(s) and one pin code is for the guests. The moderator code allows the moderator(s) to have some control over their calls. For example, the moderator can depress *5 on their touchtone phone, and this places all of the guest codes into listen only. To make everyone interactive again, the moderator would depress *5 again on his phone. Another code allows a moderator to record his conference and then place it on the bridge for other later participants to call in and listen to the call. When you sign up, we will give you a list of the moderator commands.

5. Can I have more than one set of pin codes? Yes, we can issue a set of pin codes for each person or department and bill by department also.

6. What are comparable rates from other competitors? AT&T, MCI, Sprint, and Global Crossing typically charge 4–8 cents per minute for 800 Meet Me, but you will find some older customers that are paying as much as 15 cents per minute. Some resellers charge

4–6 cents per minute. You may find some large volume customers paying less. If this is the case, ask them how many minutes they do per month, and then tell them that you will go to the president and see if he will give you a lower rate.

7. What is free conferencing all about? Free conference call providers were popular in the early 2000s, but the Federal Communications Commission has limited their revenue model severely. Several of these providers have gone out of service or started charging per minute rates. If you have important business calls, you will not want to place them on a free service, because they are overcrowded and your participants can get busy signals trying to get into your conference. With A+, you have none of these problems.

8. I would like to talk to your president directly. No problem. Let me give him your name and number and he will call you right away. Would that be okay?

9. How do I get started? I will fax or email you a half-page application. You just complete it and fax it back to 713-780-5931. We will then call you with your telephone number and pin codes and you are ready to go.

10. Can I make a call today? Absolutely. Let me get the fax or email to you.

O. Social Security Administration

www.ssa.gov

P. Suze Orman's Contact Information

www.suzeorman.com

Q. ZANY BILL FISHERISMS

Below are some of the "famous" statements that Bill Fisher made over the last twenty-seven years and that I have had the pleasure of hearing. I heard most of these sayings back in the 80s and early 90s, and some have been popularized in the national media. I am not sure where many of these quips originated, other than from Bill Fisher's sharp mind.

No Good Deed Will Remain Unpunished: Bill Fisher started using this phrase in the early 80s, long before it became part of the pop culture.

Out Where God Buried His Socks: Again, Bill used this phrase in the early 80s; it refers to something a long way off.

Out Where Jesus Buried His Sandals: This is another version of the previous one.

Washing Elephants: This refers to a person who is always planning on scoring the big deal but never succeeds.

From the Teeth Out: This is when a person tells you that he or she is going to do something but then never does it.

The Monkey Is Dead and the Show Is Over: This refers to the ultimate closure to an event or situation with someone.

It's Colder Than Kelsey's Nuts: I never knew who Kelsey was, but I am quite sure that he was a very cold fellow.

Fish Hooks in His Pocket: This refers to someone who is very cheap and never picks up any restaurant checks.

You Know, This Would Be a Good Place for a Restaurant: This phrase would be spoken to a waiter at a restaurant when Bill requested something that the waiter was unable to deliver.

The Tea Pours Like Glue: Again, at a restaurant, Bill would say this to the waiter when he couldn't get his iced tea glass refilled due to slow service.

Violating Girlish Confidences: This is when two girls, or a group of them, gossip with each other, telling each other's secrets.

When Money Walks out the Door Is When Love Flies out the Window: This one is self-explanatory.

Crime Doesn't Pay, But if It Does, I'll Take Ten Percent: Bill always said this when he heard of some news story about a crook making money illegally.

Gratitude Is the Hardest Emotion to Sustain: People are not grateful anymore. They want to ask only, "What did you do for me today?"

Your Life Changes on Seemingly Insignificant Events: Minor events sometimes lead to life-changing circumstances.

Started Well, But Farted and Fell: This refers to someone who doesn't finish.

Hotter Than a Popcorn Fart: I don't even want to think about this one.

Lips That Touch Liquor Shall Never Touch Mine: This is a silly quote by Bill.

Little Children, Little Problems; Big Children, Big Problems: This refers to the fact that little children really don't have problems compared to teenaged children.

The Harder I Work, the Luckier I Get: Usually it takes hard work—not just luck—to attain success.

Spit up His Gum: Bill said this when someone was about to hear bad or alarming news; e.g., "He is going to spit up his gum when he hears that."

Other Than the Food and the Service, Everything Was Great. This is how one might respond to a server in a restaurant: "How was everything?"

The Man Is So Tight His Shoes Squeak: This has about the same meaning as the "fish hooks in pockets" quote above.

What Does a Jewish Princess Make for Dinner? Reservations: This is an old joke.

Quit Fiddle Farting Around: This was obviously used on the Fisher children and grandchildren in the early days.

A Leopard Never Changes His Spots: People never change their behavior.

There Is No Love Without Respect: This is self-explanatory.

Always Have a Positive Mental Attitude (PMA): This is also self-explanatory.

Colder Than a Well Digger's Fanny: It's pretty cold.

Nobody Kicks a Dead Dog: This means that people of wealth and means are of great interest to others to sue, etc. However, once such people are dead or broke, others leave them alone.

Sorry, Don't Feed the Bulldog: Even though you are sorry, it doesn't fix the underlying problem.

It Is a Wise Child who Knows His Own Father: This is self-explanatory.

Winners Win and Losers Whine: This is self explanatory.

Nothing Serious: One says this in answer to "What did he die from?"

High, Hard, Outside Whirling Asshole: This is what Bill called someone he didn't like.

Three Axe Handles Across the Ass: This is what Bill called a woman with a large behind.

She Could Hunt Bears with a Switch: Bill would say this when he saw a large, muscular woman.

You Can't Put Old Heads on Young Shoulders: You can't teach young people the wisdom of older people. They have to learn for themselves.

Money Is Only Important When You Don't Have it: This is self-explanatory.

Carborundum Bastarditis: Don't let the bastards get you down.

It's Not the Fall That Kills you; It's the Sudden Stop: This one's obvious.

About the Author

Michael R. Burns had the privilege of knowing Bill Fisher, his father-in-law, for twenty-seven years. Michael observed Bill during this time and learned all of the investment strategies that Bill employed.

Michael grew up in South Texas and went to Texas A&M University. He received a BS degree in Psychology in 1970 and an MS degree in Management in 1971. After college, Michael worked for Southwestern Bell and AT&T for eleven years before founding his first company, TeleSystems Marketing, a call center business that specialized in outbound telemarketing of products/services to consumers. Michael worked in the call center industry for twenty-four years.

In 1989, Michael founded Conference Pros International, a conference service company that provided conference-calling services to businesses and nonprofit organizations. In 2000, he founded A+ Conferencing, another conferencing company that specialized in using agents and resellers to market its services.

Michael has written several articles on telemarketing and conferencing services and has written one other book, *Telemarketing: Setting Up For Success*. Michael speaks at seminars and association meetings around the country.

As mentioned in *The Boomer's Guide to Recovering Your Lost Retirement: The Bill Fisher Story*, after Bill passed away, it became apparent to Michael that Bill would be the perfect "poster boy" for Baby Boomers who had lost much of their nest eggs in the recent recession and did not know how to recover from this tragedy. Bill's three-pronged investment strategy is a great model for both Baby Boomers and seniors to help recapture their lost retirement. You can reach Mike at mikeb@nwpros.com and receive more information by visiting www.theboomersguides.com.

13961535R00046

Made in the USA
Charleston, SC
11 August 2012